Ways to the stone house   Simon Warner

All uncaptioned pictures are video stills by Simon Warner
from the exhibition *Ways to the stone house*

© The Brontë Society, 2012
ISBN: 978-1-903007-16-7
Designed by Stubbs Design
Printed by The Print Academy (Yorkshire) Limited

Contents

Introduction	5
The stone house – afterlife and inspiration, by Simon Warner	9
A tale of two houses, by Jay Appleton	17
A history of Withins, by Steven Wood	25
The South Pennine Watershed, by Robin Gray	33
Acknowledgements and further reading	48

Top Withins, 1976.
Photo: Simon Warner

4

Introduction

Wuthering Heights was hewn in a wild workshop, with simple tools, out of homely materials. The statuary found a granite block on a solitary moor...with time and labour, the crag took human shape, half rock; in the former sense, terrible and goblin-like; in the latter, almost beautiful, for its colouring is of mellow grey, and moorland moss clothes it; and heath, with its blooming bells and balmy fragrance, grows faithfully close to the giant's foot.

Preface to the 1850 edition of *Wuthering Heights*, Currer Bell.

The Brontë novels are intimately connected with the landscape of the South Pennines and the term 'Brontë Country' accurately conjures the moors and heaths that characterise this particular part of Yorkshire. It seemed therefore very appropriate that the Brontë Parsonage Museum should collaborate with the Watershed Landscape Project, a three year programme which seeks to tell the story of the Pennine uplands through partnerships with regional organisations.

Photographer and filmmaker Simon Warner has been photographing this unique landscape from his base in Stanbury since the 1970s, and was commissioned as artist in residence for the Watershed Landscape Project to create new work for exhibition at the Brontë Parsonage Museum. The resulting show, *Ways to the stone house*, was exhibited from 28 September to 3 December 2012.

Simon Warner's series of films, displayed on miniature screens and as projections throughout the rooms of the Parsonage, record encounters with natural features, vegetation and the elements on a series of walks towards Withins Height over the year of his residency. His films bring the landscape that so inspired the Brontës back into their former home. The miniature scale of the works echo the Brontës' great imaginative kingdoms contained within the pages of tiny books. Top Withins itself – the site often believed to have been the inspiration for Emily Brontë's Wuthering Heights – holds particular prominence here. Its mythic status and remote wild location has inspired generations of artists, photographers and writers, and the exhibition documents its progressive ruination during the twentieth century, seen through the lenses of early photographers as well as the loans of major works by Fay Godwin,

INTRODUCTION

Bill Brandt, Alexander Keighley and Sylvia Plath. Simon Warner collects this material together for the first time, as well as showcasing landscape photographs by groups based at Eastwood Primary School and the Bangladeshi Community Association in Keighley, taken with Simon on walks in the area during his residency year.

Jenna Holmes, Arts Officer, Brontë Parsonage Museum

William Edmondson
The Withens, (Wuthering Heights), c.1895
Photographic print
Bradford Libraries
William Edmondson was a Haworth photographer and printer between 1890 and 1936, with a shop on Mill Hey. He produced a large number of Haworth postcards.

Withens

Most people never get there, but stop in town for tea, pink frosted cakes, souvenirs, solve 42 photographs of the place too far to walk to, visiting the church of St. Michael & All Angels, the black stone rectory, rooms of memorabilia — wooden cradle, Charlotte's bridal gown of heirloom lace & honeysuckle, Emily's death couch, the small, luminous books & watercolors, the beaded napkin ring, the apostle cupboard. They touched this, wore that, wrote here in a house redolent with ghosts. There are two ways to the stone house, both tiresome.

One, the 'public' route from the town along green pastureland over stone stiles to the voluble white cataract that drops its long rag of water over rocks warped round, green-slimed, across a wooden footbridge to Heathrein goatfoot flattened grasses where a carriage road ran a hundred years back, in a time grand with the quick of their shaping tongues worn down to broken wall, old cellar hole, gate pillars opening from sheep turf to grouse country leading. The old carriage road's a sunk rut, the spring clear well & gurgle under grass too green to believe. The hulk of matted grey hair & a long skull to mark a sheepfold, a track worn, losing itself, but not lost.

The other — across the slow heaves, hill on hill from any other direction across bog down to the middle of the world, green-stained, boots squelchy — brown peat earth untouched except by grouse foot — bluewhite spines of gorse, the burnt-sugar bracken — an eternity, wildness, loneliness — peat-colored water. The house — small, lasting — pebbles in roof, names scrawls on rock — inhospitable — two trees on the lee side of the hill where the long winds come & piece the light in a stillness. The furious ghosts nowhere but in the heads of the visitors. & the yellow-eyed shag sheep house of love lasts as long as love in human mind — blue-spindling gorse

The stone house – afterlife and inspiration

Simon Warner

Can a ruin continue to have a history? Can these bones live? It is now 86 years since the last inhabitant of Top Withins abandoned his moor-top dwelling, and the shell of the building only survives thanks to periodic consolidation and strengthening. But its reputation and cultural status continue to grow, apparently in inverse proportion to the crumbling of the stones. The site is a symbolic destination: how many promises have been made there, how many ashes scattered?

The popular identification of Top Withins with Wuthering Heights has not resulted in particularly sympathetic conservation, although this connection, together with the remarkable situation of the building, explains why it has been preserved at all, when so many other moorland farms have been lost. In 1931 the house was sealed and fenced off, and until the 1950s its roof and basic outline remained intact, although repairs had to be done after vandals broke through the roof in 1935. Into the 1960s you could still admire the stepped architecture, naturally accommodating itself to the steeply falling ground. My earliest photograph from 1976 shows one wooden beam still in place, but the gable ends have already been levelled off, and its owners Yorkshire Water subsequently undertook remedial works to produce the blockhouse appearance that we see today. More comprehensive reinforcing of the reduced structure was carried out in 1997 with the approval of the Brontë Society, and in 2011 wall tops were re-cemented and stonework repointed with the help of Pennine Prospects.

The building was Grade II listed in the first Keighley Survey of 1955, a designation confirmed by statutory listing in 1974. However, after further reassessment, Top Withins was delisted in 1991 on the grounds that it had become too altered and, despite its reputed association with the Brontës, did not 'possess sufficient special architectural or historic interest to remain listed'.

In July 1997 Ann Cryer, the newly-elected MP for Keighley, raised the question of possible re-listing in an Adjournment Debate. Tony Banks, Under-Secretary for Culture, Media and Sport replied that English Heritage had made a mistake listing Top Withins in the first place. He attempted to draw a distinction between architectural and literary merit, but also said that to make any progress with relisting the Brontë Society 'must position it more accurately in the great saga of *Wuthering Heights*'.

In fact the Brontë Society had been distancing itself from the literary connection ever since 1930, when the national *Daily Chronicle* even ran an article about the shock of the Society's downplaying the links between Top Withins and Wuthering Heights. Given this history, it is interesting to consider when the Top Withins/Wuthering Heights link was first made.

In 1872 the publisher George Smith wrote to Charlotte Brontë's friend Ellen Nussey, asking whether she could identify 'the real names of some of the places so vividly described in the Brontë novels' because he was commissioning 'a skilful artist' E.M. Wimperis to illustrate a new collected edition. We do not have Ellen Nussey's reply, but a subsequent letter from George Smith thanks her for her information. The assumption that she suggested a trip to Top Withins is based on Wimperis' engraving of the moor, with Near, Middle and Top Withins in topographically accurate positions as confirmed by contemporary photographs (p.39). The only difference is that Top Withins has become a substantial house dominating the horizon.

Of course *Wuthering Heights* is associated with the whole of Haworth Moor and its environs. The novel's enormous impact has meant that sometimes just quoting the two words of the title produces an almost talismanic effect. One very striking evocation of the moor is by local photographer Alexander Keighley (1861-1947) who enjoyed an international reputation as an exhibiting photo-artist. His powerful study 'Wuthering Heights' made about 1930 (p.40) is characteristic of Pictorialism, a movement in British photography that stressed aesthetic manipulation and the deliberate creation of atmosphere. His carbon prints (as here) were heavily worked and double-printed to create an air of

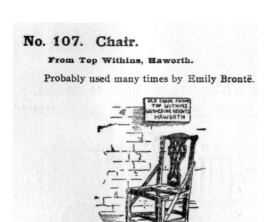

Left: Catalogue entry from the 'Wuthering Heights' exhibition at Oatlands, Harrogate, a private collection shown by J.H. Dixon up to 1916 that included many 'old things of the Brontës and Brontë Land'.

Right: Set of the lost 1920 Ideal Film Company production of *Wuthering Heights* starring Milton Rosmer. This remains the only major adaptation to be filmed in Haworth.
Brontë Parsonage Museum

mystery. Interestingly, the subject is not Top Withins but Forks House (or the constructed image of a building in roughly the position of Forks House), a long-demolished farm overlooking South Dean Beck above the Brontë Bridge.

Top Withins itself was an attraction even while still owner-occupied up to 1896, and several photographs exist showing unnamed residents or visitors. As it became a magnet for other writers, it took on more and more layers of cultural association, and most photographs deal less with its desolation than with a sense that the building retains an imaginative power. The celebrated Yorkshire author Marie Hartley photographed it in 1938 as the basis for a drawing in her 1939 book *Yorkshire Tour* (with Ella Pontefract) where she comments on walkers following in the footsteps of others who have walked this way to see the moors which inspired the Brontës.

A few years later Bill Brandt produced a photo-essay on Brontë Country for *Lilliput* magazine (May 1945) that included the pictures of Top Withins later reused in his comprehensive book about writers' houses and landscapes, *Literary Britain* (1951). It is remarkable to see these powerful photographs barely contained within the covers of a small and otherwise conventional magazine. No one has done more to reinforce the Romantic credentials of Haworth Moor than Bill Brandt, who was already well-established as a social documentary photographer but now turned increasingly to landscape, extending his technique of high contrast black and white printing to the natural world. The exhibited photograph (p.44), one of Brandt's most famous, is a combination print in which the sky has been added from a separate negative.

Above: sketch of Top Withins by Marie Hartley from *Yorkshire Tour*, based on her 1938 photograph (left).

Brandt's biographer Paul Delany suggests that a new interest in writers and their landscapes was generated by the war (people rediscovered reading) and reflected a patriotic reassessment of Britain's culture and countryside heritage. The choice of Haworth and Haworth Moor for a popular magazine also suggests a new appetite for challenging and dramatic landscapes.

In September 1956 the poet Sylvia Plath visited Haworth with her new husband Ted Hughes, and walked up to Top Withins accompanied by Ted's uncle Walt and Sylvia's college friend Elinor Friedman Klein. This must have been a significant trip for them both, as the location generated several poems over the years: three by Ted and two by Sylvia. Sylvia also drew a sketch of Top Withins (p.38) titled 'Wuthering Heights Today', showing the building in transition from house to ruin. But there are the two sycamores, constant companions to the building in all its stages of decay and still flourishing in 2012, although as Ted Hughes points out in his poem 'Wuthering Heights' from *Birthday Letters*, if they stood anywhere else they would probably be three times the size. Ted writes about taking a snap of Sylvia perched in the fork of one of the trees, and Sylvia writes excitedly to her mother about the trip:

'How can I tell you how wonderful it is. Imagine yourself on top of the world, with all the purplish hills curving away, and gray sheep grazing with horns curling and black demonic faces and yellow eyes… black walls of stone, clear streams from which we drank; and, at last, a lonely, deserted black-stone house, broken down, clinging to the windy side of a hill. I began a sketch of the sagging roof and stone walls. Will hike back the first nice day to finish it.'

In her journal Sylvia is both more analytical and more poetic:

Left: Sylvia Plath photographed at Heptonstall in September 1956, probably by Elinor Friedman Klein who recalls the trip to Top Withins when Sylvia started her sketch, and how the party got lost for hours trying to return to Heptonstall Slack over the moors.

Right: Singer Kate Bush in a BBC TV interview for *Tonight*, March 1978 before her second appearance on *Top of the Pops* with 'Wuthering Heights' at No.1. Photo: Simon Warner

'There are two ways to the stone house, both tiresome. One, the public route from the town along green pastureland over stone stiles to the voluble white cataract that drops its long rag of water over rocks warped round, green-slimed, across a wooden footbridge…The other – across the slow heave, hill on hill from any other direction across bog down to the middle of the world, green slimed, boots squelchy – brown peat – earth untouched except by grouse foot – bluewhite spines of gorse, the burnt-sugar bracken – all eternity, wildness, loneliness…'

It is interesting to see Sylvia Plath's drawing alongside Branwell Brontë's 1833 sketch of a moorland farm (p.38). This has never been identified as Top Withins but bears some of its distinguishing features.

The much-loved Haworth artist Joseph Pighills (1902-1984) painted numerous views of the villages, moor and valleys near his home in Marsh, as well as interiors and portraits. His work is in the great tradition of English watercolour. He had a particular affection for the moorland farms, but hardly ever painted Top Withins. The picture illustrated here (p.47, not in exhibition) was a commission from John and Barbara Snowden of Haworth who had to overcome his objections that it was 'on the wrong side of the valley'. The painting dates from 1976, but Pighills has looked back 20 years and reinstated the roof.

Fay Godwin's 1978 photograph of Top Withins (p.46) has become almost as celebrated as Bill Brandt's, used on book covers, exhibition posters and, for her 2010 exhibition *Land Revisited*, hung as a gigantic banner down the front of the National Media Museum. An admirer of Bill Brandt, she was included in the V&A's 1975 exhibition *The Land* which he selected, but she was also a photographic purist, coupling a very British vision to American standards of quality and finish. She always insisted on being called a documentary photographer, avoiding image manipulation and hating suggestions that her work was in any way Romantic. Fay came from the world of publishing and her first professional photographs were of writers, including Ted Hughes. It was he who suggested they work together on the project that became *Remains of Elmet* (1979), a hugely successful book celebrating and probing the landscape of the South Pennines, that (together with a revised edition *Elmet*) remained in print for 25 years. Unusually for the time, the two worked reciprocally: 'He wrote poems to go with my pictures, which in turn gave me new ideas for pictures.' Fay Godwin was famously patient in the field, waiting ages for interesting light or cloud formations. Here the ruin seems to be exchanging energy with the sky, in an image suggesting the infinite space of the unbounded moor.

Simon Warner is a landscape filmmaker and photographer with research interests in early photography and landscape history. Much of his work has been concerned with water: *The Water Babies* for Opera North Projects (Cultural Olympiad 2012), *Confluence* with Beaford Arts/North Devon Biosphere Reserve (2012) and *Seven Streams* for *The Arts of Place* (Bradford 2010). Solo exhibitions include *A Guide to Yorkshire Rivers* at Impressions Gallery and *Leaving Home* at the Brontë Parsonage Museum. Simon Warner was long-listed for the Northern Art Prize 2011-12.

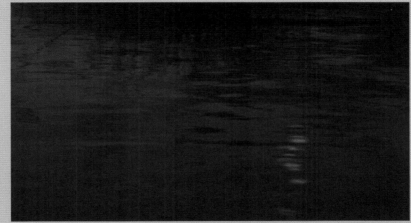

Ponden Hall, 1986.
Photo: Simon Warner

A tale of two houses

Jay Appleton

Page references are to the Penguin Classics Edition of *Wuthering Heights*, 1995

Although there is still much controversy about Top Withins and Ponden Hall as the models on which Emily Brontë is alleged to have based Wuthering Heights and Thrushcross Grange, it is the authenticity, not of the architectural details of the houses, but of their situations, which is so important, as David Cecil memorably pointed out in 1934[1] when he drew a parallel between the two houses and the dispositions of the two families, Earnshaws and Lintons, who inhabited them. The idea of landscape being an expression of temperament is articulated in the novel by Nelly when she compares Heathcliff, retiring in a sulk, with Edgar Linton, radiant in the expectation of courting Catherine. 'The contrast resembled what you see in exchanging a bleak, hilly, coal country for a beautiful fertile valley' (p.70). Again Catherine, trying to persuade Isabella of her folly, says Heathcliff is 'an arid wilderness of furze and whinstone' (p.102).

Our emotional response to the landscapes of the book is deeply influenced by Emily's word-pictures. It may help if we can find some independent yardstick against which to measure the contrasting scenes. One such yardstick is Prospect-Refuge Theory[2], a unifying theory of environmental aesthetics proceeding from the Darwinian assumption that *Homo sapiens*, like all other species, developed over millions of years a relationship between its individual members and their environment which we call a 'natural habitat'. This furnished the requirements for maintaining its lifestyle and engendered a system of attraction or repulsion which ensured that its members frequented such places as would provide the means of subsistence and survival. Such preferences may be modified by culture and personal experience, but these are never able entirely to overthrow basic instincts, like hunger, thirst, shelter-seeking, mating and many others, but above all the need to see and to hide or shelter.

The theory leads to a classification of environmental objects, conditions and even abstract concepts, based not so much on what things are like as what they mean in terms of opportunities for behavioural response. It begins with two concepts essential for survival: (1) Prospect, which includes anything to do with acquiring information, e.g. hearing, smelling or tasting, but, for our purposes, principally seeing, and (2) Refuge, which includes anything conducive to the assurance of safety or comfort, e.g. hiding, sheltering or modifying the microclimate. Since Refuge always implies 'refuge from something', we need to add a third, (3) Hazard, since we need to find out the boundary between safety and danger. Prospect-Refuge Theory, then, is a sort of shorthand phrase for a theory based on the assumption that we are creatures still largely driven by instinct to do things conducive to our survival prospects. We do them because we want to. We have now linked environmental perception with the attainment of pleasure and given hedonistic aesthetics a base in the biological sciences.

By subdividing these three categories further this simple classification can be greatly elaborated, but we have gone far enough to see that, in David Cecil's well-known summary, Thrushcross Grange is a place of Refuge and Wuthering Heights a place of Prospect coupled with Hazard, and that the dispositions of the families who live there are in tune with the landscapes.

In creating her two fictitious places, Brontë constantly gives emphasis to their respective roles in terms of Prospect-Refuge Theory by using the appropriate symbolism. Everything she says about the Grange is to do with Refuge, while everything she says about the Heights points towards Prospect or Hazard or both. Let us look at some of the passages where she does this.

The potentialities of both houses start with the situations provided by nature. Haworth and Stanbury Moors consist of wide spreads of the Millstone Grit of the Carboniferous System, gently undulating in convex and concave surfaces, some of the latter steepening into ravines where the streams have cut their way deep into the gritstone. Most of the farms in the late 1700s were in the concave depressions, even the ravines, taking advantage of the strong Refuge values derived from the shelter afforded by the encircling slopes. Many of them would have had additional support from trees (shelter belts), which were sparse on the thin soils of the open moor but grew more prolifically where the concave depressions afforded not only protection from the wind, but also more favourable rooting conditions in the higher water-table and the richer soils of the fluvial deposits of the streams. Ponden Hall demonstrates all these natural advantages and they are all conducive to Refuge.

Now look at Top Withins. It is on a conspicuous convex slope, whose shallow acid soil and exposure to the winds from all directions have inhibited tree growth. There seem always to have been isolated trees near the house, but very few in number. They had most probably been planted in the optimistic hope of producing a shelter-belt, but pretty unsuccessfully. We read of 'a few stunted firs at the end of the house' and 'a range of gaunt thorns all stretching their limbs one way' (p.4). What sort of 'refuge' would these provide? They are totally ineffective to hide behind or shelter under. Nature has therefore given both farmhouses an irreversible start in opposite directions as indicated in Cecil's summary.

So much for the reality of Ponden Hall and Top Withins. What can we learn from the ways in which Emily Brontë's imagination has built on to nature's legacy? Let us take just a few examples.

The advantages of Refuge already provided by nature were not sufficient to create Thrushcross Grange. To suit the lifestyle of the Lintons the farmyard and farmhouse garden needed to be vastly extended to Capability Brown dimensions. The distance from the gate to the house is no less than two miles (p.31). Privacy is ensured by a peripheral wall or hedge, not impenetrable, as the children discovered when they found a hole in the hedge (p.48), but seriously impeding the would-be intruder. The house is 'buried in trees' (p.205), the park gates are 'generally locked' (p.192) and the whole park is a refuge area safe enough to allow little Cathy to go on walks or pony rides on 'real or imaginary adventures' (p.192), provided she does not go beyond the encircling boundary.

Top Withins, 1992.
Photo: Simon Warner

Images of Prospect here take the form of Indirect Prospect Symbols, that is to say distant places perceived as likely to afford even wider views, such as horizons and elevated viewpoints. A horizon is by definition the further margin of a surface observable from a particular vantage-point and it plays a critical role in landscape aesthetics, as it raises questions about what lies beyond but does not answer them. Here is Little Cathy:

'Ellen, how long will it be before I can walk to the top of those hills? I wonder what lies on the other side – is it the sea?

'No, Miss Cathy…it is hills again, just like these' (p.190).

Cathy then wants to know about the 'abrupt descent of Penistone Craggs, a conspicuous elevated viewpoint, 'especially when the setting sun shone on it':

'But I know the park, and I don't know those…and I should delight to look round me, from the brow of that tallest point…' (p.190).

This is strong Indirect Prospect symbolism, and we have a dose of the Hazard when Mrs Dean, who, remember, is responsible for the child's health and safety, warns of the dangers of climbing on the Craggs. But it is all inaccessible, at least until Cathy is grown up. It doesn't threaten the security of the Grange where Brontë's terminology is overwhelmingly calculated to reduplicate the Refuge imagery bequeathed by nature.

The site of Wuthering Heights could hardly be more different. Whether or not it is based on Top Withins, everything in the text, apart from its architectural details, suggests a perfect match, and Brontë proves herself as skilful at re-enforcing the symbolism of Prospect and Hazard to create Wuthering Heights as with that of Refuge to create Thrushcross Grange. The house is in a highly conspicuous position with long views in most directions and exposure to the wind on every side. It is, of course, like all buildings, a haven of refuge, and almost every reference to the interior of a room mentions the fireplace, usually with a blazing fire. But the safety zone is so tiny, and so conspicuously segregated from the bitter weather outside that it reminds one of a cosy cabin cruiser with an artificially maintained microclimate, a capsule of comfort adrift in an Atlantic gale. References to the comparatively cosy interior merely serve to underline the contrast between Refuge inside and Hazard outside, where snowstorms, quicksands and other dangers abound. This contrast is often specifically commented on, not least to give dramatic support at critical moments in the narrative, as when the apparition of Catherine appears at the window accompanied by the sound of the branch of a fir-tree in the wind 'rattling its cones against the panes' (pp.24-5), or again, as Mr Earnshaw is dying, when 'a high wind blustered round the house, and roared in the chimney: it sounded wild and stormy...' (p.43).

If we want to know whether Top Withins could plausibly be turned into Wuthering Heights, it is not the details of the building we should be worried about but its context in the landscape. Prospect-Refuge Theory does not prove the connection, but it certainly confirms the plausibility.

The very name 'Heathcliff' is a compound of two common geographical terms. The one is suggestive of the Prospect values of wide, open views across stretches of dwarf ericaceous and other stunted plants, with sight-lines unobstructed by trees. In the other the dangerous precipices and crumbling rock faces are strong symbols of Hazard, and it is this same combination of Prospect and Hazard which so persistently distinguishes both Top Withins and Wuthering Heights.

1 Cecil, Lord David, 'Emily Brontë and Wuthering Heights' in *Early Victorian Novelists*, London (1934)

2 Appleton, Jay, *The Experience of Landscape,* Wiley, Chichester & N.Y. (1975 and 1996)

Jay Appleton is Emeritus Professor of Geography at the University of Hull. He holds Degrees from the Universities of Oxford, Durham, Hull and Heriot-Watt (Edinburgh). In *The Experience of Landscape* (1975) he proposed 'Prospect-Refuge Theory', an approach to environmental aesthetics which has greatly influenced Landscape Architecture. He is an Honorary Life Member of the Landscape Institute and Landscape Research Group. He also has seven collections of poetry with Wildhern Press.

24

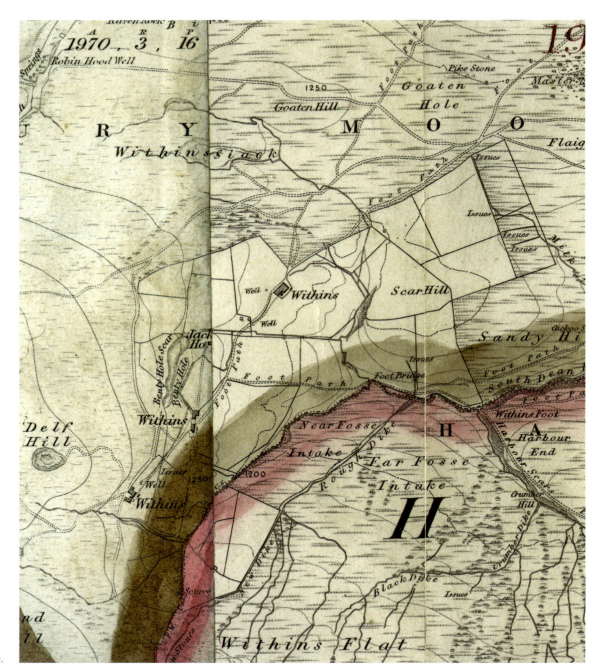

Withins Farms
6 OS 1852 b
The Withins farms and surrounding moorland from the first edition six inch Ordnance Survey map of 1852 (which was surveyed in 1847).

A history of Withins

Steven Wood

The cultivated land of Haworth and Stanbury fills low lying areas and pushes in fingers up the valleys of the River Worth and its tributary streams. In the headwaters of the Sladen Valley there is an isolated island of cultivation surrounded by unenclosed moorland. Here a hundred or so acres of meadow and pasture were farmed from the three Withins farms – Near Withins, Middle Withins and Top Withins.

Farming at Withins had started in the sixteenth century or earlier. The first recorded owners of a farm at Withins were Thomas Crawshaye and his sister Anne Crawshaye who, in 1567, sold 'sixteen acres of land with the edifices thereupon built lying in Stanbury in a certain place there called Wythens' to George Bentley for £44. This land must have been laboriously won from the moor at a time when there was a pressing need to bring more land into cultivation.

In 1591 George Bentley's descendant William Bentley divided his estate at Withins between his three sons Martyn, Luke and John. This is the earliest mention of three farms at Withins.

To avoid disagreements between the brothers William specified the rights that each was to have over the lands of his brothers. These concerned access to water, building stone and the common grazing lands. There is mention of a spring and well house on Martyn Bentley's land where his brothers were to be free to 'fetch water, wash clothes and to do all other manner of honest business'. Stone for the farm buildings and walls seems to have come from a delf on Luke Bentley's land at Wilheye. A number of other field names survive from the sixteenth and seventeenth centuries: Helywellfield, Calfheye, Cabbage, Four Nooked Close, Wynewell, Wythin Hill and Forkes Intake. Apart from the farms themselves a number of barns and other outbuildings are mentioned in this period. Most will have been close to the farms but there is mention of a barn on Within Hill in 1620: its foundations can still be seen today.

Unfortunately it has not proved possible to determine which of the brothers held which of the three farms. We do get a few hints as to the kind of farming they practised. There is mention of arable land – presumably used to grow the oats that were the staple of their diet. Most of the land would have been devoted to pasture and meadow for the support of dairy cattle.

Although dairy farming was the mainstay of these Pennine farms, those nearest to the moors also kept sheep. In the early days the wool of the local sheep would have been spun and woven into woollen cloth. When worsted weaving replaced woollen manufacture in the eighteenth century a better quality of wool had to be imported from Lincolnshire and other areas. The short stapled wool of the local sheep would then be sold to manufacturers in the woollen districts further south. Sheep are mentioned at Withins as early as 1679 when Jonas Wheelwright owned fourteen sheep worth £2. In 1723 John Crabtree had sheep valued at £40 as well as a pig and cattle, including an ox and a bull, worth £33.

Farming on the Pennine moors rarely sufficed to support a family on its own and a dual economy was practised. Around Haworth the second occupation was most often handloom weaving although some farmers worked as quarrymen. The weavers carried their pieces on their backs across miles of moorland to markets in Bradford or Halifax for sale. We know that George Bentley was a clothier and no doubt his descendants continued to spin woollen yarn and weave kerseys at Withins. By 1723 the cloth being woven at Withins was worsted rather than woollen kerseys. This is proved by the combs which feature, along with his looms, in the inventory of John Crabtree's goods.

The Bentleys sold their Withins properties in the later seventeenth century. By the end of that century Middle Withins belonged to the Lord of the Manor of Haworth William Midgley and Top Withins to John Crabtree. It is not until 1813 that we can say definitely who owned each of the three farms. In an inventory of that year we find that Near Withins belonged to George Robinson, Middle Withins to Edward Ferrand, who had purchased the Manor of Haworth from the Midgleys in 1811, and Top Withins to John Crabtree. The owners did not farm the land themselves: Near Withins was farmed by John Moore, Middle Withins by Robert Jackson and Top Withins by Jonas Sunderland.

We get our fullest picture of the Withins farms in 1850 when the Haworth Tithe Award was made. By then Near Withins was owned by Isaac Lancaster and farmed by Simeon Robinson.

Middle Withins had passed to Sarah Ferrand and was tenanted by Mary Jackson. Top Withins had been bought by Jonas Sunderland who had rented it from Crabtree.

Simeon Robinson was farming about thirty-seven acres at Near Withins. Of this ten acres was meadow and the remainder was pasture. The family at Near Withins consisted of Simeon Robinson (45), his wife Susan (43) and their ten children aged from 1 to 22. Four of their sons were engaged in hand worsted production. John was a wool-comber, Rodger and William were handloom weavers and ten year old Simeon junior was a bobbin winder. Two daughters were working in one of the local textile mills – Jane as a weaver and Susannah as a spinner. They probably walked the two miles to Griffe Mill in the valley below Stanbury village (although Ponden Mill and Lumb Foot Mill are other possibilities). All spinning was done in mills by this time and the wool combed by John Robinson would have gone to Griffe or one of the other local mills for spinning. Young Simeon wound the weft yarn onto bobbins to supply his two brothers who were working at the handlooms.

The Farms at Withins 1851
Map showing the distribution of the Withins land between the three farms. This map is based on the Tithe Map of c.1851. The reference numbers and field names are those of the Tithe Award. Near Withins has 37 acres and Top Withins has 20. Middle Withins has 34 acres of meadow and pasture and a further 52 acres of rough pasture at Fawkes Intake. The New Inn which is shown to hold 5 acres at the New Intakes is now called the Old Silent Inn.

Mary Jackson at Middle Withins had over eighty acres of land of which seventy acres was pasture and thirteen acres meadow. The only other occupants in 1851 were her son John who was a handloom weaver and her seven year old grandson James Dewhirst. Eighty acres looks like a lot of land to be farmed by an elderly woman (Mary was 67) and her son, but half the acreage was accounted for by the rough pasture of Fawkes Intake which would have needed little attention.

Land Use 1851

The map of the Withins farms derived from the Tithe Map is here coloured to show the land usage recorded in the 1851 Haworth Township Rating Valuation (RV) and in the Tithe Award (TA) where that differs. The tendency for the meadow land to be concentrated near to the farm buildings – or an isolated barn in the case of New Laith – is very obvious. This arrangement reduced the amount of work involved in getting the hay crop into the barns where the cattle were kept in winter.

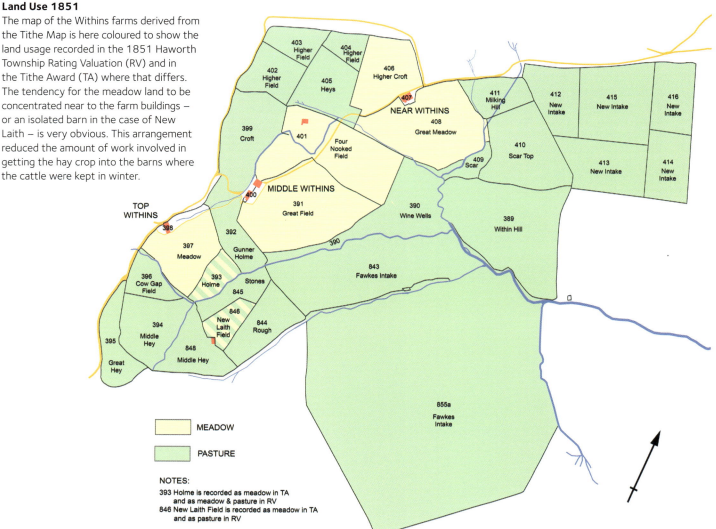

MEADOW

PASTURE

NOTES:
393 Holme is recorded as meadow in TA and as meadow & pasture in RV
846 New Laith Field is recorded as meadow in TA and as pasture in RV

At Top Withins Jonas Sunderland farmed twenty acres of which about four acres was meadow and the rest pasture. Jonas Sunderland was 45 years old and he lived at Top Withins with his wife Mary aged 46 and their children John, James and Ann. The 17 year old John was, like his father, a handloom weaver.

We can form some picture of the house at Top Withins from the inventory of the goods that Jonas inherited from his father, also Jonas, in 1849. There were five rooms: house, parlour, house chamber, parlour chamber and garret as well as the dairy and the barn. In the house (living room) were two tables, three chairs, a cupboard, a clock and various pots, pans, crockery and cutlery. There was also a copper kettle, some pewter, a lantern and a gun. In the parlour were a table, a chair, some pots and the bakestone where oat bread was baked. The house chamber had three beds and bedding, the meal chest and another chest and the families' clothes. Wool was stored in the garret along with weighing scales. In the barn were the farming tools: spades, picks, forks, shovel, scythe and a wheelbarrow.

These three families; the Jacksons, Robinsons and Sunderlands continued to farm at Withins for another forty years or so although Near and Middle Withins seem only to have been occupied for part of the year. Jonas Sunderland's daughter Ann, her husband Samuel Sharp and their daughter Mary were the last family to live at Withins.

The journalist Harwood Brierley included a description of Top Withins in an 1893 walking article for the *Leeds Mercury*: 'Here was a good specimen of a north country moorland home. It contained a fire that was not blue and smudgy, but red and yellow; while the hearth looked warm enough to mull ale or roast chestnuts. The walls were, again, blue-washed; the chairs all had tall backs: there were fully half a score lines of oat-cakes stretched across the dark ceiling: and a curious chest of dark wood fitted into an angle of the walls.' Two years later Ann Sharp died and her husband and daughter left Withins for a farm in the valley.

Top Withins was briefly occupied again some twenty years later when Ernest Roddie ran a poultry farm there from 1921 to 1926. Left unfit for his former occupation after the war he took the tenancy of Top Withins and moved in with his horse Tommy, his terrier Nell, two cats and a good supply of books. The cats thought little of the place and soon returned to the village to be replaced by two kittens who were less particular.

After Roddie left Withins the house fell into dereliction and in 1930 Keighley Corporation blocked the doors and windows to deter vandals. At the same time Near and Middle Withins farms were demolished.

Steven Wood is an independent historian who has been studying Haworth township for 25 years. He is the author of *Haworth: A Strange Uncivilized Little Place* and four books of old photographs of the area.

Eastwood Primary School mothers group outing to Penistone Hill, Haworth, May 2012.
Photo: Simon Warner

Bangladeshi Community Association seniors group geocaching at the Brontë Bridge, May 2012.
Photo: Simon Warner

The South Pennine Watershed

Robin Gray

The South Pennines Watershed Landscape is the upland area where rainwater is divided east from west; North Sea from Irish Sea; Lancashire from Yorkshire. It also marks the stories of two great watersheds in history where the impact of people changed the landscape – the arrival of agriculture and the Industrial Revolution. Written deep into this land is the story of how people lived from it and are inspired by it. Now this hard-worked landscape has a pivotal role to play in rising to contemporary challenges such as climate change.

A Cultural Landscape

To think of something as permanent as landscape being victim to something as fickle as fashion seems bizarre. But we have to recognize just how far our tastes in landscape have changed and how they might change in the future.

The romantic poets wrote about the inspirational beauty of 'untamed' countryside. Wordsworth famously claimed the Lake District as 'a sort of national property, in which every man has a right and interest who has an eye to perceive and a heart to enjoy'. They turned their backs on the aristocratic rural idyll crafted by the likes of Capability Brown, drawing inspiration instead from the beauty of wild countryside. It took the towering figure of John Muir, a Scot living in America, to make this concept real by creating the world's first national park at Yosemite in 1890. Muir talked of landscape and man's relationship with nature in spiritual terms.

It might be considered, however intuitively, that England's National Parks are in some way the purest essence of 'natural' landscape beauty; why else would the South Pennines have been rejected as being 'too industrial'. And yet, all these landscapes have been formed by man – the heather moorland, the field boundaries, the woodland – all managed whether for food, sport or minerals.

Recognition of historical context has foregrounded the concept of *cultural* landscapes. When the Peak District was designated a National Park it retained a long history of quarrying and mining, activities that formed that landscape. The 'industrial' South Pennines has an equal claim to be the historical 'watershed' between the agricultural and industrial revolution. Some argue that the traditional national park model be rejected in favour of a Heritage Area[1] – there has always been a strong vein of non-conformism in the South Pennines.

Whilst the South Pennines may not be a protected landscape, its biodiversity interest has been recognised since 1998 with a designation of Special Protection Area. The South Pennines is internationally important for ground nesting birds including golden plover, lapwing, snipe and curlew as well as breeding populations of merlin, peregrine falcon and short-eared owl. Nationally, the viability of the colonies of twite or the 'Pennine Finch', are of particular concern in the area. In England, they are almost entirely confined to the South Pennines, and numbers have been dramatically declining in recent years.

Lessons from the Past

With the time that has elapsed since our area saw significant mining, we now have a new understanding of this cultural landscape. Through the Watershed Landscape Project volunteers have been engaged in work to get a clearer picture of how the land has been shaped – on Baildon Moor for instance, where coal mining has taken place since at least the 15th century. A project called Riches of the Earth has undertaken survey work of sites at Baildon, Oxenhope and Todmorden to identify structures, embankments and quarries.

Going further back, the Watershed Landscape Project has taken cores into the peat to identify vegetation cover that predates our existing moorland vegetation. Indeed discoveries made by the University of York above Marsden provide the earliest evidence from the Mesolithic Period[2] of a primitive hunting

Left: Brontë Waterfall, May 2012. Photo: Merv Pemberton

Right: Leeds City College students Jasmine Taylor and Rebecca Stott interviewing The Stompers at Top Withins, part of a Haworth Moor visitor survey by Whitestone Arts, April 2012. Photo: Simon Warner

culture. Depressions in the peat have been interpreted as a fire pit with shards of flint from the process of preparing arrowheads.

On Ilkley Moor volunteers have surveyed over 400 carved rocks dating from the Bronze Age to help their long-term conservation and aid our understanding.[3] What transpires is a relationship between man and his environment that is forever dynamic. Not necessarily always one of harmony, indeed there are theories that communities would have moved after a landscape had been used beyond its capacity to sustain hunting or fuel. Are these lessons that we need to comprehend for the future?

The future

'It is not commercialized and it hasn't been ruined – you could shut your eyes and it wouldn't have changed in hundreds of years.'

Perhaps another lazy assumption would be that our landscapes are somehow a metaphor for tranquillity, even consensus. We should shatter that illusion; the founding of the National Parks resulted from a social movement that included the notable mass trespass on Kinder Scout in 1932. Those arguments between private rights and the common good continue today in different fields; the tension between shooting rights and conservation on grouse moors; the desire to protect cherished views versus the demands of urban populations for water, for renewable energy…for recreation.

Increasingly we are being asked to consider the 'utility' of our natural environment and even to put a value on its 'services'. To put a value on landscape has drawn bitter debate, but in an increasingly

Left: Ian Blane cementing the wall tops at Top Withins, October 2011.
Photo: Simon Warner

Right: Rhododendrons below Moor Lodge in the upper Worth Valley, June 2012.
Photo: Nazia Asif

urbanized world it is true to say that the unintended consequences of *not* valuing our natural environment has caused a legacy that we are only now beginning to recognize. Think of how the smoke from the chimney stacks of industrial Manchester was carried on the wind to deposit its toxic legacy on our moors. Areas of bare peat that took thousands of years to form can be eroded by anything up to a metre in a matter of decades. Bearing in mind that 70% of our water supply comes from our uplands, the problems of peat erosion cost millions of pounds for utility companies to address. Add to this years of over-grazing, wildfires and drainage in a misguided attempt to boost agricultural production on 'marginal' land. No wonder that the uplands have been the scene of a call for action with organisations such as Pennine Prospects, Moors for the Future and Yorkshire Peat Project at the fore.

Community engagement

Whilst clearly there are those who value this landscape and those you would expect to value it, what about those who do not? Perhaps the realisation that this landscape is necessary every time a tap is opened can change the value placed upon it. To this end the Watershed Landscape Project working with Groundwork, an environmental charity and Kidz Arch, an archaeological consultancy have brought the story of the South Pennines to over 50 schools and over 2,000 schoolchildren looking at subjects from water supply to 'what is peat'. The project has also commissioned three visual artists and three writers in residence to bring this story and this landscape to those who might not otherwise experience it. For example, poet Char March worked with Thorne Park Deaf School to explore the moors using senses other than sound. Photographer Simon Warner teamed up with Groundwork to bring a group from the Bangladeshi Community Association to Haworth Moor. Overall the artists have worked with 400 different individuals drawn from over 20 organisations, schools and community groups.

Landscape value

What value can be placed upon a landscape that has inspired artists and writers from the Brontës to Ted Hughes? With this in mind Pennine Prospects sought to establish what it is that people valued about our countryside. The results of these focus groups, brought together by the company Research Box, were illuminating; perhaps there is no better testament to Wordsworth's sentiment than how visitors are still inspired by our landscape:

'It is the wildness and I don't know if it is because we are from the north but it is ours. It is not like the Lake District.'

'When I am sat there nothing can get to me, no-one can bother me but anywhere else it can. When I am sat there I hardly get anyone walking past. It is just de-stressing.'

'I come here for the solitude. Occasionally you don't want to see anyone else. It is escapism, time to think. It is like freedom somehow.'

'My wife asks me, "What do you think about when you are up there?" and I say "Nothing", that's the point!'

'I feel uplifted, I don't know if it is spiritual. Contemplation maybe.'

Here in the South Pennines, the Watershed Landscape Project has sought to ensure that key landmarks are conserved, even if not restored. The iconic ruin of Top Withins may or may not be Wuthering Heights but nonetheless it is valued by thousands of visitors. Using Heritage Lottery Funding it has been made good against the Pennine weather and a shooting lodge on Turley Holes has also been restored. Over sixty volunteers have learnt drystone walling. These high altitude structures remind us of the livelihoods hard-won from the moors.

1 A proposal championed by Pennine Heritage that gained national profile for a South Pennine Heritage Area.
2 Spikins, P.A. (2003) *Nomadic People of the Pennines: Reconstructing the Lifestyles of Mesolithic People on Marsden Moor*, West Yorkshire Archaeology Service and English Heritage.
3 Spikins, P.A. (2011) *Research Agenda for Palaeolithic and Mesolithic sites in West Yorkshire*, WYAAS Available at: www.archaeology.wyjs.org.uk/documents/archaeology/Palaeolithic-and-Mesolithic-Research-Agenda-for-West-Yorkshire.pdf

A landscape architect working for Pennine Prospects, Robin Gray has managed the Watershed Landscape Project since 2009. The Project has recently been shortlisted for the National Lottery Awards in the environmental category.

Branwell Brontë
Moorland buildings
Pencil on paper, 1833
Brontë Parsonage Museum

Sylvia Plath
Wuthering Heights Today
Pen and ink on paper, 1956
Collection: Bel Mooney

Edward Morrison Wimperis
Wuthering Heights
Engraving in 1872 collected edition of the Brontë novels, published by Smith Elder
Brontë Parsonage Museum

Moorland Track to Withens, showing the three Withins farms, Photographic print, c.1910
Brontë Parsonage Museum

40 Alexander Keighley
A Derelict Moorland Farm, Haworth, Emily Bronte's 'Wuthering Heights'
Carbon print c.1930
© Royal Photographic Society/NMeM/Science & Society Picture Library
On loan from the National Media Museum, Bradford

Cecil George Waudby
Haworth ramblers with Middle and Top Withins in background
Digital print from scanned glass negative, 1912
Brontë Parsonage Museum

41

J.J. Stead
The Withens, Haworth Moor
Photo-mechanical print, c.1905
Brontë Parsonage Museum

Edward G. Malandine
Scar Hill, Haworth Moor
Silver gelatin print, 1945
Brontë Parsonage Museum

Published in *Illustrated* magazine, 19 January 1946. E.G. Malandine was a photographer on the *Daily Herald* before and after WWII, during which he served as an official photographer for the War Office.

Bill Brandt
Top Withens after Emily Brontë
Silver gelatin print, 1945 (reprinted 1975)

Image © Bill Brandt Archive
On loan from the Victoria and Albert Museum

Simon Warner
Beams and Sycamores at Top Withins
Silver gelatin print, 1978

Fay Godwin
Top Withens, Near Haworth, Yorkshire
Silver gelatin print, 1977
Image courtesy of British Library
On loan from the National Media Museum, Bradford

Joseph Pighills
Top Withens
Watercolour, 1976
Collection: John and Barbara Snowden

Acknowledgments

Simon Warner and Jenna Holmes would like to thank Pennine Prospects and Bradford Museums and Galleries for their financial and practical support of the exhibition, symposium and residency. We would like to thank Ann Dinsdale, Collections Manager at the Brontë Parsonage Museum, for her kind expertise and for providing exhibits; also Steven Wood for his encyclopaedic knowledge of Haworth township, and generous assistance with the Top Withins display.

Special thanks to Karen Kukil, Associate Curator of Special Collections, William Allan Neilson Library, Smith College, Northampton, MA for providing Sylvia Plath material from the Smith collection.

We thank owners and copyright holders for permission to exhibit and/or reproduce the following:

Bill Brandt *Top Withens after Emily Brontë*
On loan from the Victoria and Albert Museum
Image © Bill Brandt Archive

Fay Godwin *Top Withens, Near Haworth, Yorkshire*
On loan from the National Media Museum
Image courtesy of British Library

Alexander Keighley *A Derelict Moorland Farm, Haworth, Emily Brontë's 'Wuthering Heights'*
On loan from the National Media Museum
Image © Royal Photographic Society/NMeM/Science & Society Picture Library

Sylvia Plath's drawing of Top Withins is exhibited and reproduced by kind permission of Bel Mooney

Photograph of Sylvia Plath, and Sylvia Plath's journal page exhibited by kind permission of Smith College

Sylvia Plath texts © Sylvia Plath Estate

Joseph Pighill's painting of Top Withins is reproduced by kind permission of John and Barbara Snowden

Further reading

Lucasta Miller *The Brontë Myth*, Jonathan Cape, 2001

Ann Dinsdale, Sarah Laycock and Julie Akhurst *Brontë Relics: A Collection History*, The Brontë Society, 2012

Alexander Keighley: A Memorial, Royal Photographic Society, 1947

Ella Pontefract and Marie Hartley *Yorkshire Tour*, J.M. Dent, 1939

Bill Brandt *Literary Britain*, Cassell, 1951

Paul Delany *Bill Brandt: A Life*, Jonathan Cape, 2004

Intro. Frieda Hughes *Sylvia Plath – Her Drawings*, The Mayor Gallery, 2011

Ed. Karen Kukil *The Journals of Sylvia Plath 1950-1962*, Faber & Faber, 2000

Ed. Aurelia Schober Plath *Letters Home by Sylvia Plath: correspondence 1950-1963*, Faber & Faber 1975

Nobbut a Bit o' Mucky Watter: A Tribute to Joseph Pighills, Bradford Art Galleries & Museums, 1985

Ted Hughes *Birthday Letters*, Faber & Faber, 1998

Ted Hughes and Fay Godwin *Remains of Elmet*, Faber & Faber, 1979

Ted Hughes and Fay Godwin *Elmet*, Faber & Faber, 1994

Fay Godwin *Landmarks*, Dewi Lewis Publishing/Barbican Centre, 2001